Contents

Some words are shown in bold, **like this**. You can find out what they mean by looking in the glossary.

What is a waterfall?

It has been a long, stormy winter. The mountains are covered in snow.

In springtime, the snow begins to melt. One by one drops of water trickle out of the ice, creating a small stream. As more water feeds the stream, it grows and runs faster, moving downhill.

Eventually the stream runs into a large, swollen river. Soon it is tumbling and churning, bringing a powerful flow of icy water with it.

A mountain stream becomes Skogafoss Falls in Iceland.

Skogafoss Falls, Iceland

Suddenly the ground beneath disappears. The rapidly flowing river falls freely as a beautifully arching **waterfall**. The water pounds down on the rocks far below.

A steep drop

Angel Falls in Venezuela is the world's tallest waterfall. It drops 979 metres (3,212 feet) before finally crashing onto the ground below.

Angel Falls, Venezuela

For many years, people have known about the power of falling water. They have found ways to capture this energy and turn it into **electricity** that we can use in our homes and factories.

The power of falling water

Anyone who has seen **waterfalls** up close knows how powerful they can be. Water starts at the top as a gently flowing river. But, by the time it reaches the bottom, that same water seems to be an unstoppable force of tumbling and churning white water.

Victoria Falls is one of the world's most famous waterfalls.

Victoria Falls, Zimbabwe

The force (strength) of the water is caused by **gravity**. Gravity is a force on Earth that pulls everything down towards Earth's surface. The farther the water falls, the more powerful the force.

Where does the energy of the water come from? It comes from the Sun. Warm sunlight heats the water in oceans and lakes. This energy causes the water to evaporate (turn into a gas) and rise into the air. The energy is released when the water falls back to Earth as rain. The water continues to lose energy as it pours down mountains and over cliffs, falling to the lowest point it can reach.

Yosemite Falls, United States

Yosemite Falls in the United States drop over 700 metres (2,297 feet) from the high mountains to the valley floor.

Early uses of water power

Water has been used for power for thousands of years. The simplest early device was a **waterwheel**. This is a wheel that is pushed by flowing water. The turning wheel is used to power machines and do other work. By using water power, the work done by a person or animal was reduced.

The first waterwheels were used by ancient Greeks and Romans, as far back as 240 BCE. They were used for grinding grains, getting water to villages, and **irrigating** (watering) crops.

As early as the 1st century CE, a waterwheel was used in ancient China to grind grain and create iron. Soon these wheels were put to even more uses, including rotating an instrument used to study the stars.

This drawing shows a waterwheel in ancient Egypt.

In Europe after the year 1000 CE, waterwheels became even more popular. There was much work to be done, but not enough people to do it. **Mills** were built to put the energy of flowing rivers and streams nearby to use. Mills are machines (or buildings with machines) that use waterwheels to convert flowing water into power. People during this period used mills to make paper, grind grain, flatten cloth or paper, and crush objects.

A historic waterwheel in Omagh, Ireland.

Many European countries have used waterwheels for power.

The waterwheel

The **waterwheel** developed over time, but most waterwheels share the same basic features. Most are made of wood or metal. The wheels often have blades or buckets on them to catch the water that will turn the wheel.

As water heads towards the wheel, it is channelled through a gate. The gate helps to keep the water flowing smoothly against the wheel.

If the wheel has buckets, they fill with water on one side of the wheel. As the buckets are filled, the side with water becomes heavier. This extra weight turns the waterwheel. Waterwheels with paddles or blades are set up in fast-flowing water. For these waterwheels, the force of the water running against the paddles turns the wheel.

The blades of a waterwheel help the wheel to turn.

As a waterwheel turns, it also turns a **shaft** (a kind of bar) attached to the wheel. This shaft powers a machine that does the work, such as grinding grain.

This diagram shows how a waterwheel uses water power to grind grain.

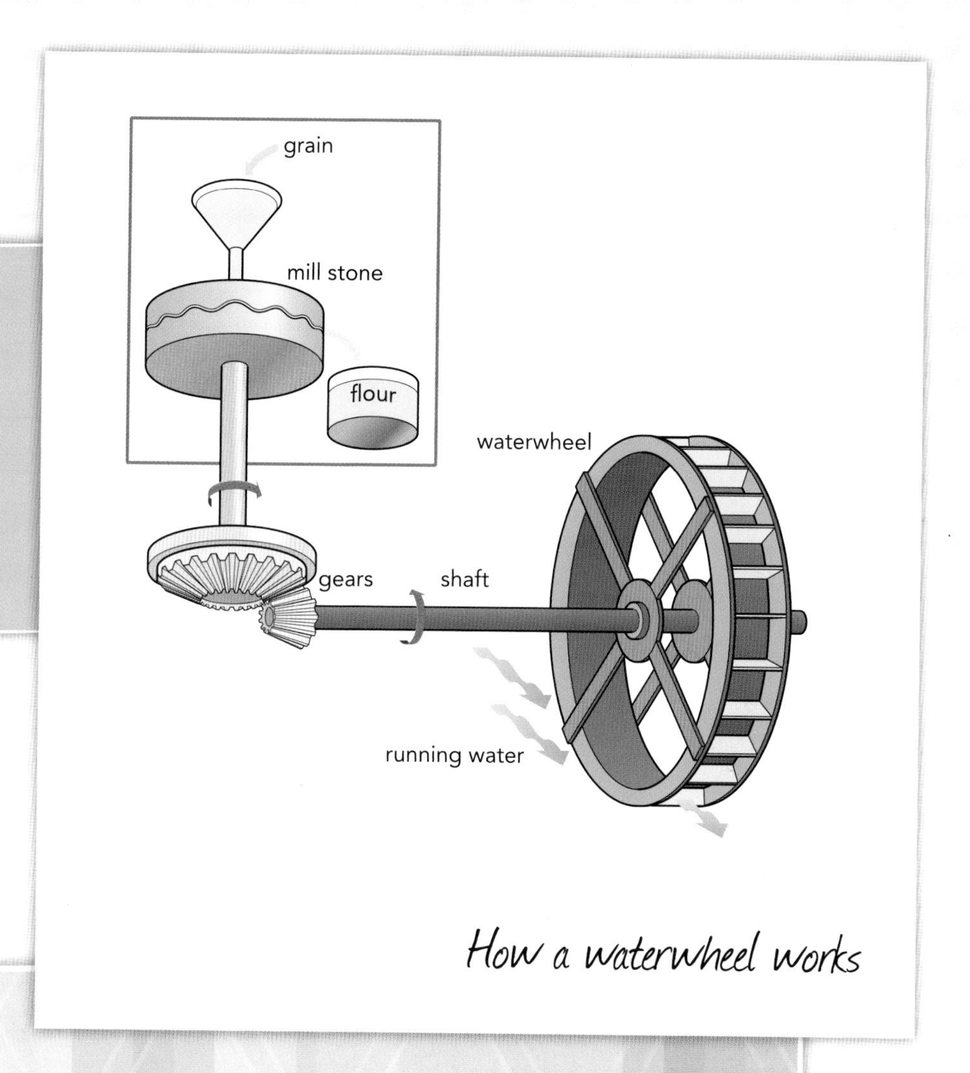

How a waterwheel works

Barony Mill

Barony Mill in Orkney is still in use today. In the winter months it is used to grind grain. In the summer people can visit the mill to see how it works.

Building a dam

Waterwheels are built along a flowing river or stream. But rivers and streams are not always dependable. Sometimes they can flow heavily. Other times they can be just a trickle.

To make the flow of water steady, sometimes people create a **dam**. A dam blocks the river so that lots of water can build up. Then the water is slowly released at an even pace.

Kariba Hydroelectric Dam, Zimbabwe

Kariba Dam was built to store water for people to use, as well as to produce **electricity**.

The water that builds up behind a dam creates a human-made lake called a **reservoir**. The reservoir can be used for flood control, fishing, boating, or **irrigating** crops.

The Three Gorges Dam is part of the world's largest **hydroelectric plant**.

Three Gorges Dam, China

Three Gorges Dam

Along the Yangtze River in China is the world's largest dam. The Three Gorges Dam, completed in 2006, is the largest concrete structure in the world. The dam created a reservoir that is 660 kilometres (410 miles) long. Unfortunately, the reservoir flooded the homes of millions of residents, forcing them to move away.

It's electric!

Today, the power of water is used to make **electricity**. A place that does this is called a **hydroelectric plant**.

Hydroelectric plants are usually built near the bottom of a **dam**. Being at a lower level helps these power stations use the force of falling water. Water held back by the dam pours steadily into the plant. The water is channelled through a pipe called a penstock. Penstocks are set up to help control the flow of water.

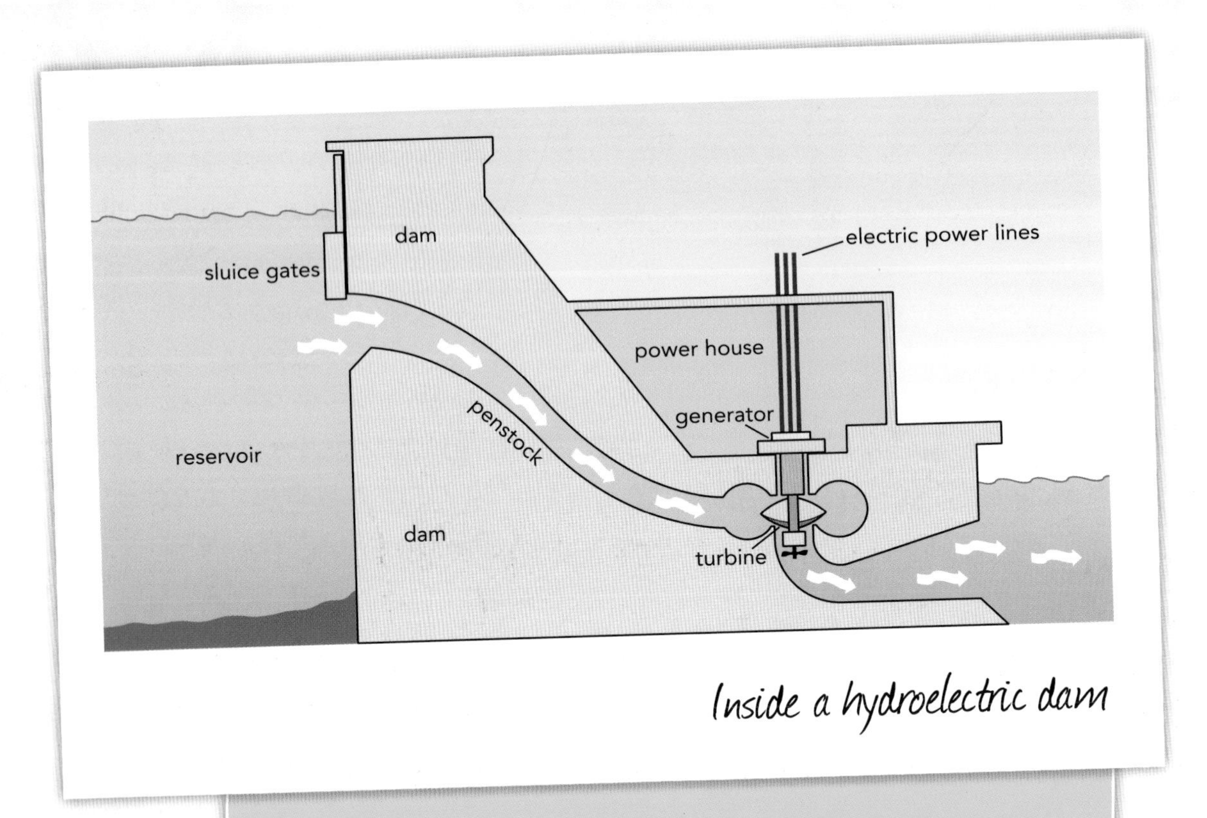

Inside a hydroelectric dam

Hydroelectric stations are located at the lower end of dams and **reservoirs** to let **gravity** increase the power of the water.

Next, the water pours over the blades of a **turbine**. The pressure of the moving water turns the blades, making them spin like a windmill. Then the turbine turns a **generator**, making electricity. Once the water passes by the turbine, it continues out of the dam and moves downstream.

Huge generators like these are found inside hydroelectric plants.

Turbine generators

A bright start

In 1882 in Wisconsin, USA, a **waterwheel** was set up on the Fox River. The energy from the waterwheel was used to provide light to a paper **mill**, a house, and a building nearby. This was two years after inventor Thomas Edison had created the light bulb, so electric light was an exciting new concept. This waterwheel was the world's first hydroelectric plant.

Electricity in our homes

The water power that spins a **turbine** eventually becomes **electricity** that lights our homes. But how does this happen?

When water spins a turbine, it turns a **shaft** that is connected to a **generator**. The generator is what makes electricity. The round rotor, which contains magnets, spins inside the generator. Spinning magnets create electricity in the stator, a metal piece that surrounds the rotor. Wires inside the stator carry the electricity out of the generator.

Moving water makes the turbine spin. This spinning energy is turned into electrical energy in the stator.

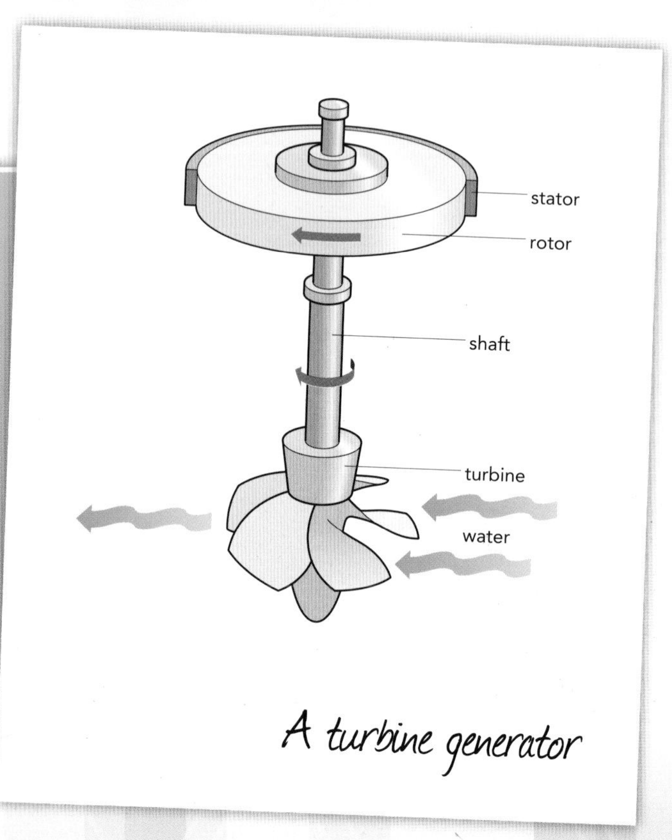

A turbine generator

The electricity travels through the wires to a power system. From there, power lines carry it all over the country. The electricity is then turned into power for homes and factories.

These power lines are part of the grid system bringing electricity from plants to homes.

The biggest yet

A planned **hydroelectric** station is in the works on the Red Sea in the Middle East. When it is built it will be the world's biggest hydroelectric **plant**.

Who uses water power?

Kurobe Dam is the largest dam in Japan. It is 186 metres (610 feet) high.

Kurobe Dam, Japan

The five countries that use the most **hydroelectric** power in the world are China, Canada, Brazil, the United States, and Russia. Norway, India, and Japan also get lots of electricity from water.

Canada gets more of its electricity from water than any other country. In fact, hydroelectric **plants** are so common there that many Canadians refer to any power plant as a "hydro".

What places are good for creating water power? Areas with lots of rain or snow will have more flowing water. Also, rivers that travel from high to low areas are more powerful. These are the areas where hydroelectric stations will be found.

The United Kingdom gets about 2 per cent of its electricity needs from water. Out of the total renewable electricity used in the UK, 40 per cent comes from water.

Famous hydroelectric plants

Hydroelectric dams are in use all over the world. Here are a few famous ones.

Niagara Falls

This beautiful **waterfall** is on the border between the United States and Canada. Niagara Falls is a famous tourist attraction. Since 1893 some of the water has flowed through a hydroelectric **plant** instead of over the falls. It is a source of power for thousands of people.

Around 12 million tourists visit Niagara Falls every year.

Niagara Falls, Canada and the United States

Aswan High Dam

The Aswan High Dam in Egypt also uses water for power. Lake Nassar, behind the dam, is the largest human-made lake in the world. This body of water also supplies drinking water to Egypt. While doing that, it makes 10 billion kilowatts of power for the country every year.

Itaipú Dam

The Itaipú Dam in Brazil is on the Paraná River, close to the famous Iguassu Falls. It is part of the world's largest hydroelectric plant. The plant provides **electricity** to Brazil and Paraguay.

It took 30,000 people to build the Itaipú Dam.

Itaipú Dam, Brazil

A huge waterfall

There are 275 waterfalls that make up Iguassu Falls, spanning almost 3 kilometres (2 miles).

The Hoover Dam

The Hoover **Dam** in the southwest United States holds back water from the Colorado River, creating Lake Mead. This **reservoir** is the largest human-made lake in the United States.

It took less than five years to build the Hoover Dam.

Hoover Dam, United States

The dam, named after President Herbert Hoover, was built in the 1930s. It is an arch-**gravity** dam. This special type of dam curves out into the water, pushing the water to either side. The water on the sides presses on the sides of the dam, helping to hold it together.

A huge structure

When it was first completed, the Hoover Dam was the largest electrical station in the world and the world's largest concrete structure. It is 221 metres (726 feet) tall and 201 metres (660 feet) thick.

The Hoover Dam has a **hydroelectric** station. There are 17 electrical **generators** on site to create **electricity**. When the station is at full power, it can create enough power for 750,000 people! It is the 35th-largest hydroelectric station in the world.

Other types of energy

Water power is not the only way to create **electricity**. Here are a few others.

Fossil fuels

Fossil fuels are found in the top layer of Earth, called the crust. These are made up of the remains of tiny plants and animals. Fossil fuels, such as coal, oil, and gas, can be burned for power. Most of the world's energy comes from these fuels.

Solar energy

People can collect energy from the Sun and convert it to **solar power**. Because there is always sunlight, solar energy can be replaced by nature. This type of energy is called renewable energy. Solar power can be used to heat water, provide lighting, and more.

Solar energy plant

Power from the Sun is an alternative to burning fossil fuels.

Nuclear power plant

Nuclear power is another way to get electricity without using oil, gas, or coal.

Nuclear energy

Atoms are the smallest parts of an element. (An element is the most basic part of a material.) When they are split or fused (joined) together, they release energy. This energy can be used for power. **Nuclear power** makes up about 15 per cent of the world's electricity.

Wind energy

Wind can be used for power. Wind **turbines** spin with the wind. These connect to a **generator** that produces electricity. Large wind farms have turbines set up in breezy areas. **Wind power** right now makes up 1 per cent of the world's electricity.

The benefits of water power

The world is running out of **fossil fuels** such as coal, oil, and gas. These fuels take millions of years to form. When we use them up, they will be gone forever.

This oil production platform takes oil from Earth's crust under the sea.

Water, however, is always with us. The water that is used to create energy goes back into oceans or lakes. It can one day be used again.

A water **plant** lasts longer than a coal plant, so people can use it longer. Water power also uses fewer workers, making it cheaper to run.

Water is a constantly renewable source of power.

Water power is cleaner than many other fuels. Burning fossil fuels causes **pollution**, meaning chemicals get into the air, soil, and water. It also contributes to the heating of the planet, known as global warming. **Nuclear power** leaves behind toxic (poisonous) waste, which can be very hard to get rid of. This dangerous waste must be buried underground for many years.

Hydroelectric power, however, is much cleaner and less dangerous. There are other benefits to hydroelectric power. A **dam** can be used to control flooding in an area that was once dangerous to live near. The **reservoirs** formed can also be used for fishing and swimming.

Water-power problems

Water power does have some problems. **Hydroelectric** stations can cause harm to the animals in an area.

Salmon need free running rivers without dams to return to their birthplace to spawn.

Salmon are one type of fish affected by **reservoirs** and **dams**. Salmon must return to their original birthplace up rivers and streams to spawn (lay eggs). Passing through **turbines** along the way can harm them. In some cases fish ladders have been built to help the salmon swim over the dams. A few dams have even been torn down so that salmon can return to spawn where they were born.

Dams change the rivers downstream from them. Floods that once deposited **sediment** or soil useful for fish living in the river no longer occur. Dams also release water from the bottom of a lake into areas downstream. This water may be colder and have less oxygen. Many fish die because of this. It also may alter the way people use the river – such as whitewater rafting.

Sometimes dams for hydroelectric power can get clogged with mud. This can make the water bad for drinking. The water must be cleaned, which is expensive.

Although making electricity from water may not work for all regions of the world, it will probably be used more and more often in the future.

Glossary

atom smallest part of an element (the most basic part of an object)

dam structure built to hold back and store large amounts of water

electricity energy made for powering anything from lights to appliances to factories

fossil fuel coal, oil, and gas used for energy

generator machine that makes electricity

gravity force or weight of objects due to their attraction towards the centre of Earth

hydroelectric related to hydroelectricity, which is when water is used to generate electricity. Hydroelectricity is often associated with a large power station.

irrigate bring water from one area to another through channels and pipes

mill machine (or building with machines) that uses waterwheels to convert flowing water to power

nuclear power using the energy made from the splitting of atoms to create power, such as electricity

plant place where a product such as electricity is generated

pollution when human-made chemicals get into the air, soil, or water

reservoir large human-made lake created by building a dam

sediment rock, sand, and dirt that has been carried to an area by wind, water, or a glacier

shaft bar that is connected to devices that move or rotate pieces of equipment in order to do work

solar power using the energy of the Sun to create power, such as electricity

turbine device with spinning blades that powers a hydroelectric plant

waterfall steep drop in a river's or stream's course that causes the water to fall directly downwards

waterwheel wheel that turns by using the force (power) of flowing water. The energy created is used to power machines and do other work.

wind power using the energy of wind to create power, such as electricity

Find out more

Books

Do you still have questions about how falling water is made into electricity? There is much more to learn about this fascinating topic. You can find out more by picking up some of these books from your local library:

Water and Geothermal Energy (Fuelling the Future), Elizabeth Raum (Heinemann Library, 2008)

Water Power (Energy Debate), Louise and Richard Spilsbury (Wayland, 2007)

Water Power (Energy Sources), Neil Morris (Franklin Watts, 2008)

Websites

The history of the use of water is found on this site:
www.waterhistory.org

For a complete list of the world's best waterfalls, their location and size, go to:
www.world-waterfalls.com

To learn more about hydroelectricity, visit the British Hydropower Association's website:
www.british-hydro.org

This site is all about power from water, including hydroelectricity, tidal power, and wave power:
www.nef.org.uk/greenschool/documents/WaterPower.pdf

Index